Not Your Father's Retirement

By

Ken Mahoney

ISBN 978-0-9980047-0-9

This publication contains the opinions and ideas of the author. It is sold with the understanding that neither the author nor publisher is engaged in rendering legal, tax, investment, insurance, financial, accounting, or other professional advice or services. If a reader requires such advice or services, a competent professional should be consulted. References to organizations have been given for the purpose of information and do not constitute a recommendation. Any perceived slights of specific people or organizations are unintentional.

No warranty is made with respect to the accuracy or completeness of the information contained herein, and both the author and publisher specifically disclaim any responsibility for any liability, loss or risk, personal or otherwise, which is incurred as a consequence, directly or indirectly, by the use of any of the contents of this book. While the information and advice in this book are believed to be accurate and true at the time of publication, neither the author, publisher or distributor can guarantee results nor accept any responsibility or liability for any damage or losses of any kind resulting from any advice included in this guide, be it from the author, any person or persons mentioned in this book, or any product, listing or mention, whether directly or indirectly.

The mission of Mahoney Asset Management

Know our clients well

Anticipate their needs

Exceed their expectations!

Contents

About The Author – Ken Mahoney

Investor, author of 7 books including *A GPS for Your Retirement*,  and licensed financial advisor for more than 27 years, Ken Mahoney is the CEO of Mahoney Asset Management where he offers clients tailored retirement solutions. Using data provided by the leading financial research companies, Morningstar and Standard and Poor's, Mahoney Asset Management provide detailed performance analysis and investment recommendations for goals like preparing to leave your job, purchasing a second home, or planning for retirement.

Because of Ken's comprehensive financial expertise, he is sought after by CNBC, Fox Business News, ABC and The Today Show to speak on topics such as planning for retirement and stock market investment strategies.  Ken has also been a staple on morning, drive time radio, providing financial advice for the past 24 years to listeners in the local New York City Market and can be found on America's Weekend, a financial radio program that is syndicated to over 1500 radio stations throughout the country. Having been recruited to serve on the House of Representatives Banking and Financial Services Committee, he advised the Chairperson of the Committee, Congresswoman Sue Kelly, on the impact of new financial regulations, Federal Reserve Bank transparency, and guided the Committee in asking questions of Alan Greenspan.

A believer in giving back, Ken has been serving his community for more than two decades volunteering as a member of Meals On Wheels and The United Way. Ken is the former Chairman of the Board at Make-A-Wish Foundation, and currently serves as chairman of the alumni board. Acknowledged by the New York State Legislature for his dedication and outstanding community service, Ken was honored with a Distinguished Service Award and chosen by Rockland County as community leader of the year.

In addition to his work as a financial advisor and community leader, Ken is a successful Broadway producer and investor. Ken won the Tony Award of Best Revival of a Musical as producer of *Pippin and Gershwin's Porgy and Bess*, and was nominated for a Grammy Award for producer of the Best Musical Theater Album *Matilda* and *Nice Work*. Ken is also a three time Emmy Award winner for his work as producer on the television show *Due Process*.

Ken and his wife Trish have been married since he proposed to her in 1994 on the ice skating rink under Rockefeller Center Christmas tree. They have two sons, Brendan and Connor, for whom Ken coaches' baseball and soccer. When not working for his clients, Ken can be found writing and reading several books per week like *The Snowball Warren Buffet and the Business of Life*; *Shark Tales*; and *David and Goliath: Underdogs, Misfits*, and the *Art of Battling Giants*.

Preface

I've been helping people to retire for nearly 27 years. In dog years, that's roughly 189! So, needless to say, I have seen it "all" when it comes to financial planning for the future - or in some cases, no planning at all.

Yet, one common theme that seems to ring true in many of the meetings that I have with clients is them telling me that they wish they had their dad or mom's pension. I always have to remind them that today, it's not your parent's retirement anymore - and because of that, a different approach must be taken in order to be successful.

Any more, only certain types of employers such as municipalities offer defined benefit pensions for police officers, fire fighters, teachers, and other select positions. Alternatively, nearly all of the large Fortune 500 companies offer a 401(k) plan - not a pension, like they did for your parents and grandparents. In these plans, it is up to the employee, not the employer, to ensure that you have enough saved for retirement.

Even many of the telephone companies, such as AT&T and Verizon, that once offered pensions have converted their pensions over into 401(k) plans. In just a generation, companies have essentially placed the responsibility solely on their employees to make defined contributions into plans such as

401(k) and 403(b) plans, and are no longer responsible for ensuring their workers' ongoing income in the future. This is why it is absolutely essential to have your own retirement plan in place - and why we've developed a GPS system, along with solutions to combat the issues of ensuring that you have the retirement income that you will need.

The concepts that are discussed in this book are not simply just "theories," but rather tried and true facts - because the changes in how we retire have been true for my family, too. My own father worked as a union sheet metal worker. When he retired, he had a pension and an annuity. My grandfather worked at Fleischmann in Peekskill and passed away at a young age. My grandmother worked at Reader's Digest and received income from a work pension/annuity that paid her until the day she passed.

But today, things are different. Even though just one and two generations ago my family could rely on the income from pensions, we now have 401(k) plans. Even at Mahoney Asset Management, we have a 401(k) plan. And, if our plans aren't properly funded, as well as supplemented with additional sources for retirement income, you and I may all run the risk of running out of income at a time when we need it the most.

While we miss our "father's retirement" of defined benefit pension plans, there is some good news now, too. For example, in my father and grandparents' examples, there were no cost of living adjustments. They also had skills that were not easily transferable to other opportunities - especially once they got into their 60s.

Today, there are many people who can enjoy "mini" retirements, or "serial" retirements, which I have identified examples of in this book. I have watched many of my clients retire, only to "un" retire, as they want to be more engaged and feel a sense of purpose in their "second act." In the second act of life, doing what you enjoy is key, while for many people, making income is secondary.

Just as everyone who is traveling on the highway is going to different places, everyone's idea of the ideal retirement will also differ. This is why having the retirement GPS system is so important. There is no one-size-fits-all plan. For that reason, our GPS system, will provide you with your own personalized projection.

At the end of this book, there is a questionnaire that will help you to determine your specific GPS coordinates. I can't think of a better tool to see where you are, where you are going, and what steps you need to take - right now - to get you there.
We hope that the following chapters will help you in this new paradigm of "it's not your father's retirement."

*Note: *While the concepts in this book are helpful, they are general in nature. For a more personalized plan, contact us. We run several promotions each year, where these GPS projections are free of charge.*

The retirement of today, and that of the future, has changed dramatically from what it used to be - especially over the past 25 years. Gone are the days of working for just one employer, receiving a gold watch and a handshake, and being assured that income will last throughout your "golden years."

Retirement today isn't your father's retirement - and because of that, it has to be planned for differently. What may have worked years ago won't work today, tomorrow, or years into the future - and the best time to start planning for this new retirement is now.

One of the biggest catalysts of this change has to do with the economy itself. Back in the "old days," more people worked at manufacturing jobs and spent their whole careers with just one employer. Now, we are more service based, and people are much more apt to change jobs more frequently.

In fact, according to the U.S. Department of Labor, the average person in the U.S. who was born between 1957 and 1964, had to go job hunting an average of 17.2 times between the time they were age 18 and age 48.[1]

This changing of jobs - or even of entire career paths - can have a major impact on how, and how much, is being saved for the future. It can also have an effect on when a person is even able to retire at all.

Today, people are also more likely to work after they retire. This could be in the form of volunteering, starting a brand new business endeavor, or moving into a different career that they've always wanted to try.

Pensions Are Disappearing

Another key reason that people need to change the way they plan for retirement is the fact that defined benefit pensions are disappearing. In the past, many companies used the defined benefit pension plan as their retirement plan of choice. These plans, as the name suggests, pay out a set amount of income benefit to their recipient upon retirement. The amount of this benefit is determined by a formula that takes into account the employee's salary history, as well as his or her length of employment.

For those who participated in a pension plan, the employer would promise to pay out a set, guaranteed amount of retirement income for life - and because of this, the liability of the pension plan rested solely with the employer, not the employee. Oftentimes, 100% of the contributions that went into the pension plan were also made by the employer as well.

Throughout the years, due in large part to the expense of keeping pension plans afloat, many companies have done away with defined benefit pension plans and have replaced them with defined contribution plans. The most popular of these is the 401(k).

In a defined contribution plan, the benefits that accrue are directly attributed to the deposits that are made into an employee's account - plus any gains. The funds that are contributed will typically come from the employee through salary deferrals, and possibly a small additional amount through an employer's matching contribution.

For the most part, though, the defined benefit pension plan will soon be long gone. In fact, most people who work outside of government employment cannot count on a defined benefit pension plan at all.

Private Sector Workers Participating in Employment-Based Retirement Plans

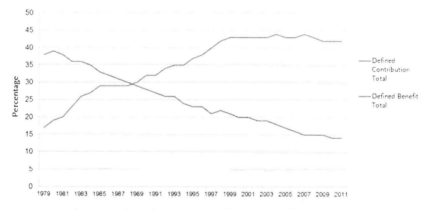

Source: Employee Benefit Research Institute

The Three-Legged Stool Retirement Model is Teetering

Traditionally, retirement income has primarily come from three key sources - pensions, Social Security, and personal savings. These sources are often referred to as the "three-legged stool." In the past, income from the combination of these three sources was usually more than enough to support retirees throughout their retirement years.

But now, due in large part to many changes that are taking place such as disappearing pensions and longer life expectancies, these sources may no longer provide enough to maintain your intended lifestyle - especially for the number of years that you may live. For example, even though Social Security retirement benefits do usually make up at least a portion of many retirees' incomes, according to the Social Security Administration, these benefits only replace about 40% of an average wage earner's pre-retirement wages now.[2] In addition, there has been a great deal of uncertainty regarding what will happen with this program in the future.

People Are Living Longer

Another key factor that is changing the way we plan for retirement today is our longer life expectancies. While living longer can certainly have its advantages, it also presents many challenges - especially in terms of stretching out savings.

According to LIMRA, a worldwide association of insurance and financial service companies, half of retiree couples are likely to have one spouse that will live to age 90 - and one in 4 may have a spouse that will live to age 94.[3]

With excellent health status, 25% of retirees can live to age 97, and in one out of eight retiree couples, either or both of the spouses will live to celebrate their 100th birthday![4] With that in mind, it is essential to have income that lasts as long as we do. Unfortunately, yesterday's planning strategies may not meet today's and tomorrow's income needs.

What's Your Dream?

Close your eyes for a moment and imagine your ideal retirement. What do you see? Are you relaxing in your new beach home? Or, does your dream take you somewhere else, like hiking through a state park, playing golf, or volunteering for a favorite charity? Your retirement dream can be as varied and unique as you'd like it to be - and rightly so - because you've worked hard for it. That's why, when saving for the future, you need to have a dream to go with it. Our dreams can, in essence, help us to define where it is that we want to go. It has often been said that once we define our "why," the how comes much more easily.

Options are Now Varied for What You Will Do After Your Primary Working Years

Today, retirees have many more options available in terms of what they can do after their working years have passed. You may decide to continue working part-time, or turn a hobby into a business. You may even decide to take some time off for a while, and then go back into the work force. The choices are literally unlimited. But, in order to have these options in your control, it will be important to have worked your plan.

Certainly, being able to retire will require that you have enough funds to pay your living expenses without having income from an employer. But having a truly successful retirement will also mean that you are following your dream.

In retirement, you will create the purpose behind how you spend each and every day - and because we are living so much longer now, many of us will have the opportunity to live in retirement for 20, 30, or more years.

But in order to do so successfully, without worry that income will run out, it will require that you are able to align your retirement dream with the financial wherewithal to support it - and that requires you to map out and to follow a detailed roadmap that will take you to your destination.

Today, it's not your father's retirement - it's yours. So you will have to plan accordingly. But by getting - and staying - on the right path, you'll be able to do just that.

Sources

1. Bureau of Labor Statistics. U. S. Department of Labor, Economic News Release, "Number of Jobs Held, Labor Market Activity, and Earnings Growth Among the Youngest Baby Boomers: Results from a Longitudinal Survey Summary. March 31, 2015. http://www.bls.gov/news.release/nlsoy.nr0.htm

2. Social Security - Understanding the Benefits. Page 4. http://www.socialsecurity.gov/pubs/EN-05-10024.pdf

3. The Retirement Income Reference Book, page 78. Copyright 2012.

4. Ibid.

Chapter Two: How Can You Know Where You Are Going Without a Map?

When people think of retirement, any number of varied ideas can come to mind. This is because retirement can be a unique and different journey for everyone - and what may be important for one person to work towards may matter very little to someone else.

That is why having a plan that is geared towards your specific needs is so essential, because just simply stashing away money in account and "hoping for the best" really isn't a very good strategy. A much better option for getting you where you want to go is using a detailed map - one like the GPS Method.

I frequently hear from retirees who did not take the time beforehand – as you are doing now -- to think through how you will spend your retirement days that they feel like the Bill Murray character in the 1993 movie "Groundhog Day." In the film, Bill Murray lives the same day over and over again, and you can get stuck in a similar loop in retirement. That could be having to contend with the same financial problems over and over again because you did not plan adequately. Or your days could be spent in an uninspired monotony of a few familiar activities because you lack the means to do the things you dream of. Your retirement can be much more satisfying if you stop now to consider what would be most meaningful to you and take steps to achieve it.

The GPS Method

The GPS Method is essentially like getting the big picture view from 30,000 feet so that you can obtain a clear overview of where you're going, and then plot a more detailed, step-by-step course on how to get yourself there. This can entail assessing your investments, evaluating downsizing, seeking other potential sources of income, and even knowing when it may be time to sell various assets. But without this type of planning, having just basic ideas of retirement are abstract. Once you make an actual plan, though, you will be much more assured of moving forward - and you'll also have the confidence that you can get there.

How to Get There from Here - GPS Analogy

Have you ever planned a 2-week long vacation to a place that was far away, but yet not looked at a map before you got in the car and started driving? Doubtful. It just simply wouldn't make any sense. How would you know where you were going - in fact, how would you even know which direction to start out?

Now, what about planning a 20 or 30-year long vacation without first looking at a map of where you were going? Sounds pretty silly doesn't it? But the reality is that many people "plan" for their retirement that way. Sure, they may be saving money for the future - and they may even be setting aside a sizeable chunk in their employer-sponsored retirement plan, in an IRA account, and/or in personal savings and investments. But if you don't have a clear cut direction for where you want to end up, then how do you know if your investments are performing like they're supposed to be - in fact, how do you know if you're even invested in the right financial vehicles for you at all? The answer is that without a clear cut plan in place - *you don't*.

Planning for the Destination

The beauty of creating your own roadmap is that no two journeys are exactly alike. The GPS Method isn't a "cookie cutter" approach. Because retirement is such a unique journey for everyone, with this approach, you can decide where you want to go and how you want your future to look. Then, once you've determined your ultimate destination, the GPS Method will help you in creating a plan that will get you there.

Think about your retirement, and then ask yourself these questions:

- Where would you like to live?
- How will you spend your day?
- Will you travel?
- Will you have a second home?
- What goals would you like to accomplish?
- Do you plan to work part-time or volunteer?
- Will anyone else depend on you for income or support?

The way that you spend your time in retirement can have a substantial impact on the future of your finances - and the time to start planning for that is right now.

You've probably heard it said that most people will put more time towards planning a two-week vacation than they do planning their own retirement. But by just taking an hour every couple of months and looking at your GPS plan, you can see if your retirement projections are on track, and whether or not you need to make any adjustments. In fact, with the GPS Method, once your plan has been set up, it takes very little time at all to keep the plan intact and running smoothly, ensuring that the financial vehicles you have chosen to take you to your destination are still performing as you had anticipated.

Looking at the Big Picture

The GPS Method starts with a "top down" approach. It takes a look first at the big picture overall, and then breaks it down into more specific individual strategies for what you need to do in order to get there. In some cases, you may have various "gaps" in your current plan - gaps that may otherwise have gone unnoticed without having a detailed projection for how to get you to all of your intended future goals. The GPS Method finds those gaps, and helps you to fill them in.

The GPS Method isn't just a way to plan financially - rather, it offers a whole new way to think about planning for your financial future. By providing a step-by-step map for you to follow, this system offers investors more confidence in that the retirement that they hope for will actually come to be - and because of this, it tends to spark a much more positive attitude overall as you move through the phases of your plan. This can carry you forward, even during times of market turmoil and volatility, as you'll know that it is only a temporary setback.

Using the GPS Method, planning for retirement can also become a much more interactive way of ensuring that your future becomes the one that you hope it will be, rather than something that will be an unknown until you actually get there. Unfortunately, those who have no true plan in place for their retirement can oftentimes only "guesstimate" what their lifestyle will be like when - or if - they are finally ever able to leave the world of employment.

Alternatively, having an actual plan provides you with a way to not just know where you are going - but to actually set the course. Having your own personal GPS will also help to keep you on track so that you *stay* on course with your plan.

Today, there are a myriad of ways that investors can be thrown off the course to their initial destination. You may also find that, due to various life changes, you'll be required to take some detours along the way. But, being prepared for these can help you to be financially ready for such things so that you'll be less likely to be knocked off course and better prepared to deal with certain risks. Some of the key risks that you can be faced with along your route may include:

Key Risks

- **Inflation Risk** - While everyone knows that prices of goods and services tend to rise over time, what is more difficult to put into perspective is just how much that can affect your income in retirement - especially if you spend many years living on a fixed income. This is because inflation lowers the purchasing power of your money - and even a slight level of inflation can take a significant toll on what you'll be able to spend on items down the road.

  As an example, an average inflation rate of just 3.22% can cut your purchasing power in half in just a 20-year period of time. This means that your income would have to double what it is today in order to purchase the very same goods and services in 20 years that you buy right now. In other words, if you're spending $3,000 per month today on items to live on, in 20 years, your investments would need to be generating $6,000 per months - just to keep pace with inflation. With a good plan, though, you can factor inflation into the mix, and ensure that your future income rises over time in order to help keep pace with your increased expenses.

- **Order of Returns Risk** - Order of returns risk is a danger that not many investors are aware of - but it is extremely important to be knowledgeable of this, and to plan it for as you approach retirement. This is because order or returns risk can have a major impact on the amount of income that you have in the future, as well as in how long your money will last.

Throughout our working lives, investors are often told that short-term market fluctuations don't really matter, as long as the overall return is positive. However, once you retire - and even within the few years leading up to retirement - that all changes substantially. This is because a "down" year in your portfolio can have a long-term negative effect on your income and your assets going forward. It can also cause you to run out of money in retirement much faster. As an example, two investors each start out with $100,000 in their portfolios, and each of the investors uses a 9% withdrawal rate for his income withdrawals. Likewise, each of the investors has an average overall return on the portfolios of 7%. However, because Investor A had a negative return in Year 2 as opposed to in Year 3, his portfolio runs out of money six years earlier that Investor A's does - with all other factors being equal.

Investor	Year 1	Year 2	Year 3	Ave. Return	Years Until Depleted
A	+7%	-13%	+27%	+7%	18
B	+7%	+27%	-13%	+7%	24

Source: Government Accountability Office, June 2011.

Given that, it is essential that once you begin taking withdrawals from your portfolio, you are mindful of not just the annual returns on the portfolio, but also the *order* of those returns, especially in the early years of the withdrawals.

- **Market Risk** - Market risk is something that most investors fear - especially if they have lost money in a volatile market in the past. Today, the market still shows some signs of instability - and unfortunately, even a small market "correction" could have an effect on your portfolio within a very short period of time. This is why it is essential to have assets that are properly diversified and allocated, based upon your goals, your risk tolerance, and your stage in life. The GPS Method essentially removes this fear from planning - because the plan that you are following is the one that's right for *you* - not a "one size fits all" plan, or worse yet, just a smattering of investments that are scattered here and there.

31

- **Longevity Risk** - Today, people are living longer life spans than ever before. Yet, even though that is great news, it can actually make maintaining an ongoing lifetime income extremely difficult. There are a couple of reasons for this. First, you need to stretch out your savings for a much longer period of time. Many years ago, retirees didn't have to worry about this. Because life spans were shorter - and because retirees could often rely on the income that they received from pensions and Social Security - income from personal investments was typically just a supplemental or a secondary source. Now, however, things have drastically changed. With the fast disappearance of defined benefit pension plans, coupled with the uncertainty of Social Security, retirees are relying more and more on income from personal savings.

  The issue is compounded, though, by the fact that our longer life spans means that these savings must often be stretched out to last for 20 or 30 years - sometimes even longer. And during this time, your money is still subject to all of the other risks - inflation, order of returns, and market risk. So, not only are you subject to financial risks, but longer life spans means that we are subject to all of these risks for a longer period of time, too.
  In addition to that, longer life spans will also mean that many of us are subject to an additional financial risk - the

need for health care and long-term care. According to Genworth's 2014 Cost of Care Survey, the average cost of just one year in a skilled nursing home facility (private room) was more than $87,000. At that rate, how long would a long-term care need take to deplete your savings? With a good plan in place to help protect your assets, you may not have to worry about it. That's where the GPS Method can help.

Don't Wait Too Late

One of the most important components to the GPS Method is ensuring that you don't wait until it's too late to implement your plan. Sometimes, when you're traveling to a particular destination, and you've discovered that you're on the wrong road, it's easy to turn around and get back on track to where you're supposed to be.

In other cases, though, no matter how hard you may try, if you realize the error too late, chances are that you just aren't going to make it. That's why there is no better time to begin implementing your plan than right now, before it's too late to put into place the strategies that are needed to get you where you want to go.

How to Figure Out How Much You Can Count On

The GPS Method isn't a do-it-yourself endeavor, but rather it allows you to use a trusted guide so that investors are not on the journey all alone. Using its proven worksheets and guidance, investors know exactly what needs to be done in order to reach their goals.

By planning ahead, you can help yourself to ensure that you are moving towards the lifestyle that you want to have in retirement - and that you won't just end up "getting whatever you get" when you arrive there.

Having a plan that encompasses your goals and your financial resources can get - and keep - you on the proper path. It can also help you to avoid the media hype and all of the other potential distractions that can end up throwing so many investors off their course.

The Information You Will Need to Gather

As you create your overall plan, you will need to first gather some information in order to get you started. Just as with any other journey, you should pack accordingly the tools and items that are necessary for the trip. For the GPS Method, these tools will include the following:

- Employer-sponsored retirement plan statement(s) (i.e., 401(k), 403(b), SEP IRA, SIMPLE IRA, etc.)
- IRA balance(s) Information - Traditional, Roth, or both

- Personal Investment balances such as stocks, bonds, mutual funds, etc.
- Personal Savings balances
- Social Security Statement - Projected future income amount
- Other Retirement Income Sources (i.e., Annuities, Rental Income, etc.)
- Insurance Coverage(s) - Life Insurance, Long-Term Care Insurance, Disability Insurance, Medicare)

Once you have incorporated the necessary data, you will have your starting point.

Next, you will need to determine where it is that you want to go. For example, some important questions that you will also need to answer include:

- When to you want to retire (i.e , at what age)?
- How much (anticipated) income will you need for your monthly living expenses in retirement?
- How long will you need that income to last?
- How much will need to go towards taxes as versus net spendable income?
- How much will you need to have saved in order to meet your long-term financial goals?

It's important to keep in mind that the GPS Method is not a short-term endeavor, but rather a long-term journey. With that in mind, there will be peaks and valleys. Just as with any long journey, knowing what to expect ahead of time can always make the trip much easier. So, prior to moving forward, it is important to be in the proper mindset.

A good, positive attitude will go a long way in helping you to achieve your financial goals - especially during those times when the road may get bumpy. So, once you've got all of the tools that you need properly loaded into your GPS system, buckle up and let's get ready to move forward.

GPS Retirement Goals Worksheet

Today, it's much easier to get anywhere than it was many years ago. With the help of services like GPS devices, we are able to get - and stay - on course, and we can even take the appropriate detours if there are any obstacles or roadblocks along the route. Having our own personal "map" can truly help to guide us to exactly where we want to go. By adding in the specific details regarding where we are now and what our ultimate destination is hoped to be, we can oftentimes not only plan the most direct route to where we're trying to arrive, but also some alternate courses just in case of a change along the way. This is where the Retirement Goals Worksheet can help. With this worksheet, you will fill in the goals that you have for the future, as well as the additional details. You will your own worksheet folded inside this book, to help you with your own GPS.

While we would all like to meet our financial goals quickly, the reality is that doing so is really a long-term endeavor. Certainly, there are stories of those who have "hit it big" by choosing just the right stock at just the right time, but these are few and far between.

In most cases, slow and steady wins the race. But the good news is that if you set good, solid, and realistic financial goals, and then commit to them, you will be able to get where you want to go.

The first step in the journey, though, is getting yourself into the proper mindset.

The Power of Your Thought Patterns

Throughout your life, you may have heard someone tell you to be careful of what you think. While many people shrug this off as just a cliché, the truth is that, there is a lot more power in our thoughts than what most people might believe. In fact, the power in our minds is one of the strongest and most useful powers that you possess.

There's an old saying that states, "What we think about, we bring about." Oftentimes, this statement can hold true in terms of our thoughts determining our success, our failure, and even our overall direction in life.

Our thoughts can actually be like a little video that plays on a screen inside your mind. Whatever it is that you have playing there can actually determine the kind of experiences that you have, and the kind of life that you live. Therefore, in order to make any changes in your life, you will need to "play" a different video. This can start with setting and committing to certain goals.

Setting Goals and Intentions

To truly be able to achieve financial success, you will need to set financial goals - and be committed to them. Your goals can be short, intermediate, and long-term. For example, short-term goals are those that you want to accomplish within the next 12 months. You may, for instance, want to pay off your car loan by the end of this year.

Intermediate-term goals are those that you would like to accomplish within the next five years. An example here could be that you want to save for the down payment on a new home. If you would need approximately $24,000 for the down payment, then you could set a goal to save an extra $400 per month for the next 60 months (5 years).

$$\textbf{\$400 X 60 months = \$24,000}$$

Long-term goals are those goals that will take longer than five years to accomplish. For most people, being able to retire with enough income to live on comfortably is a common long-term goal. In order to do so, you would need to have saved a certain amount of money to generate that income by a certain age. Once you have set your goals, you can't just let them sit and gather dust. Actually making them a reality will require that you commit to maintaining control over your spending, your debt, your income, and your savings in order to achieve them. And, even though you will likely face some financial challenges along the way, the more committed you are to your goals, the more successful you will be at attaining your desired results.

What Worries You - Moving from Fear to Solutions

A major detour to achieving one's financial goals isn't necessarily always a volatile stock market or not having enough money to put into savings or investments. Rather, it is fear. According to Warren Buffett, who is thought by many to be the greatest investor of all time, there are actually four fears that may hinder investors at any given time. These include:

- **Fear of Loss** - The fear of losing money can end up keeping investors from even moving forward with a particular trade or investment. Alternatively, it can also keep an investor from selling a losing position - ultimately causing them to lose even more. The solution to this particular fear is to have patience before buying into a position and being realistic about the investments that you get into.

- **Fear of Missing Out** - By being fearful of missing out on "the next big thing," this fear keeps many investors constantly checking the market. In turn, this can cause an investor to over-trade, and to constantly shuffle their positions. Unfortunately, this can end up costing them in high broker commissions and fees - which essentially eats into their return. Here, you need to create your plan - and then stick with it.

- **Fear of Letting a Profit Turn into a Loss** - With this fear, an investor will hurry up and sell an investment that has a gain - only to miss out on additional gains in the future. The solution here is to always have a risk-adjusted profit target in mind prior to entering into an investment.

- **Fear of Being Wrong** - This fear tends to follow investors who allow their emotions to drive their trades, not the market, the probabilities, or even just common sense - and this can be quite costly. Unfortunately, these investors will oftentimes hang on to a losing investment longer than they should just so that they can be "right," even though they know they should cut their losses and sell.[1]

What Are Your Priorities?

In addition to setting goals, it is also important to know what your priorities are - and to stick with them. For example, as you work your financial plan, are you going to focus more at this time on eliminating debt, building up an emergency fund, or setting aside money for a down payment on a home?

While having several different goals is important, it is equally as important to know which of those goals you will be focusing on at a particular time. Otherwise, if you have too many goals that are competing against each other, your plan could fall apart.

Figuring Out Who to Trust

It is helpful as you work through your plan to have a trusted advisor to rely on. Yet, in today's world, it can be difficult to know who to trust. When seeking a financial advisor to work with, then, it is important that you ensure that they are the right fit for you - and that they are also well qualified to do the job.

There are several questions that you should ask a potential advisor up front, such as:

- How long have you been in the financial services business?
- Where did you obtain your training?
- What is your investment philosophy?
- Which licenses do you hold?

- Do you have any additional certifications or designations?

You may also want to simply talk to a potential advisor to see if you get along with them personally. Oftentimes, working with a financial professional will be a long-term commitment, so you will want to work with someone whom you not only trust but also are comfortable with.

The Right Mindset

Having the right mindset is absolutely essential to your financial success in both the short- and the long-term. Just like any other type of goals that you're trying to achieve, it all begins in the way that you think.

The way you think about money can determine a great deal about where you will end up financially. For example, your thoughts can actually dictate your feelings about what is - and what isn't - important about finances. And, they will also determine your attitude, and in turn your motivation, regarding your discipline in terms of sticking to a regular savings and investment plan.
While just simply thinking about money won't automatically bring you wealth, visualizing and then behaving in such a way that you can imagine yourself accomplishing certain financial goals can get you going in the right direction.

Analysis Paralysis

One of the biggest hurdles that keeps investors from moving forward and accomplishing their goals is "analysis paralysis." Wikipedia defines analysis paralysis (or paralysis by analysis) as being a type of "anti-pattern," or a state of over-analyzing - or over-thinking - a situation so that a decision or action is never taken, in effect paralyzing the outcome.

When a person over-thinks a situation, even the most simple of situations can appear to be complicated - and because of that, the sheer quantity of the "analysis" can essentially overwhelm you into not making any decision at all. This can be harmful to your investing, because it essentially means that you will end up doing nothing at all when you should be taking steps forward towards accomplishing your financial goals.

In many ways, analysis paralysis can be thought of as being the opposite of "extinct by instinct." which refers to making quick, hasty judgments that are based solely on gut reactions. This, too, can be harmful to your financial goals.

Retirement Goals Worksheet

Today, it's much easier to get anywhere than it was many years ago. With the help of services like GPS devices, we are able to get

- and stay - on course, and we can even take the appropriate detours if there are any obstacles or roadblocks along the route. Having our own personal "map" can truly help to guide us to exactly where we want to go. By adding in the specific details regarding where we are now and what our ultimate destination is hoped to be, we can oftentimes not only plan the most direct route to where we're trying to arrive, but also some alternate courses just in case of a change along the way.

This is where the Retirement Goals Worksheet can help. With this worksheet, you will fill in the goals that you have for the future, as well as the additional details.

Sources
1. How Buffett Beats the Four Fears of Investing (http://www.nasdaq.com/article/how-buffett-beats-the-four-fears-of-investing-cm402943)

In order to arrive successfully at your desired destination, you will need to enter the proper coordinates into your GPS device. Just as with going on any other type of journey, even if you make just one wrong turn, though, it could throw you completely off course. So, when initially setting up your overall plan, it will be important to ensure that you have all of your options in place.

This also means properly preparing for your journey prior to getting in your vehicle and "turning on the engine." In other words, before you really put the petal to the metal with your savings and investing, you may need to consider paying down any major debt that you have that is holding you back.

Otherwise, if you're carrying a high-interest debt load, the payments that you are making every month could be offsetting any amounts that you are setting aside in savings for your future. It will also mean taking a good hard look at what you're spending every month.

Drill Down Into Spending

The first order of business is to analyze how much you are spending each month on your living expenses. These expenses will include the necessities such as housing and food, as well as the non-essentials like fun and entertainment.

If you find that you are spending more each month than you are bringing in, then it's time to sit down and consider where you can trim back. For example, there are many areas that can likely be cut – without even being noticed or creating a hardship in your life.

Take, for instance, if you have premium cable channels and / or an unlimited package for data on your cell phone. By cutting back on these services, you could essentially save upwards of $100 per month – which comes to $1,200 per year.

You could also be smart consumer by being mindful of sales and items with coupons. Even if you are able to save $20 per week by doing so, this can save you in excess of $1,000 per year ($20 X 52 weeks = $1,040).

You may also decide to say home and rent a movie rather than going out. This can save you a great deal of money – even if you only do so once per month. Considering the cost of a movie ticket and popcorn, you could essentially save at least $50 per couple each month.

Although each individual item in and of itself may not appear to represent a lot, when added together, they can represent a great deal of overall savings – savings that can be put towards your future. These funds could also be put towards paying down any large debts that you may be carrying.

Get Out of Debt

If you are holding on to high-interest credit card debt or other similar obligations, it is essential that you rid yourself of these as soon as possible. Oftentimes, the credit card companies charge interest rates that can exceed 20% - and if you don't pay off your balance each month, this can add up quickly.

By eliminating this debt, you can not only rid yourself of an additional monthly payment, but you will typically raise your credit score. And, the money that you were using to pay off this debt can then be shifted over and put into savings.

Estimating What You Will Need

In planning for your financial future, you will have to get an estimate of how much you will need in terms of living expenses in retirement. Certainly, most people will have some type of housing expenses such as rent or mortgage, as well as utilities and food. When reaching retirement, though, there are some costs that may go up and others that may go down in comparison to what you are spending now. For example, you may not spend as much eating out after you retire, as you will be able to stay home and cook more meals. Conversely, many retirees have increased healthcare costs – especially due to their increasing age.

With this in mind, getting a better idea of how much you will need in retirement for living expenses can help you to further develop a budget – and from there, a total amount of savings that will be needed in order to generate the income you need can be determined.

Major Expense Categories

In retirement, just as during your working years, you will have several major expense categories. These will include the following:

Housing

One of the largest expense categories in your retirement expense budget will be for housing. Regardless of whether you opt to own or rent your residence, you will need to allocate a certain amount to go towards this budget item.

Included in this category will also be:

- Utilities
- Maintenance and upkeep
- Insurance
- Property Taxes (if applicable)

Healthcare

The largest expense that most retirees will encounter is that of healthcare. Due to increasing age, the need for healthcare typically goes up over time. Costs to anticipate in this category can include items such as basic check-ups and wellness visits, as well as maintenance and control of certain illnesses, prescription medications, and potential long-term care costs.

Many retirees rely on Medicare for their basic healthcare needs. However, while Original Medicare (Part A and Part B) covers a wide array of circumstances, it also tends to leave a lot of "gaps." These come primarily in the form of coinsurance, copayments, and deductibles. In order to help in paying for some of these out-of-pocket expenses, many retirees will also purchase a Medicare Supplement insurance policy.

One area where Medicare covers very little – if anything at all – is long-term care. Because of this, long-term care insurance can be purchased to help in paying for a variety of care needs, ranging from care in a skilled nursing home facility, an assisted care living facility, and care in a recipient's own home.

By having many of these expensive needs covered through insurance, you won't have to worry about unexpected costs eating away at your retirement nest egg – or about having substantially large bills coming in that can raise your monthly budget to an unmanageable level.

Taking Care of Others
In addition to your own care, it is possible that you may need to take care of someone else during your retirement. That being the

case, you will need to include a certain amount into your budget for care giving.

You may have to provide care to an ailing spouse or significant other – or, because people are living so much longer today, it could be that you will have to provide care to an ailing parent (or parents) during your retirement years.

Dreams and Fun
In addition to the necessary expenses like housing and healthcare, you will also want to allocate some amount into your retirement living budget for dreams and fun. After all, retirement should be about having fun – so be sure to include a certain monthly amount into your anticipated budget for travel, golf, or whatever it is that you intend to do during this relaxing time in your life.

You Might Be Surprised That You Can Spend More Than You Think

Once you have developed your anticipated budget for retirement, add up the amount that you will need as your total. Based on that total – and the amount of expenses that will decrease as versus what you are currently spending – you might be happily surprised to find that you will be able to spend more than you originally thought.

Whatever your number has come to, though, the next step in the journey is to determine a method of creating an ongoing income stream for you. That way, you will be able to comfortably retire, knowing that you will have an income, month after month, arriving for you, so that you can enjoy the retirement lifestyle that you have created.

When we dream of our ideal retirement - regardless of whether that entails traveling to far away countries, relaxing on a sunny beach, or playing 18 holes of golf each and every day - one thing that will be a common thread in order to keep the engine running is an ongoing retirement income source.

While you may have spent many (or all) of your working years saving for your future, when you eventually reach that longed-for date at the employment finish line, you will need to convert those saved dollars over into a well-oiled machine that will continue to generate income for you, month in and month out, throughout your retirement years.

The question is, will you have enough income to support the lifestyle that you've been dreaming of? If not, the time to fix that is right now, either by saving more money, or by planning to either postpone your retirement date and / or to work at least part-time during your retirement years in order to fill in the income "gap."

Creating an Income Stream

Once your paycheck stops from your employer, it is likely that you will still have bills coming in each month from a number of different sources that will need to be paid. Just because someone is retired and is no longer "earning" income by working every day doesn't mean that they no longer use electricity, put gas in their cars, or purchase food from the grocery store.

That being said, it will be important to ensure that when you make that leap from being an employee to being a retiree, you have a livable income in place - and one that will hopefully last you for many years, given today's much longer life expectancies.

Traditional Income Source - Social Security

Social Security has been a staple for providing retirement income to many - if not most - Americans for roughly 80 years. This federal program was designed to protect both individuals and their families from the loss of earnings due to retirement, as well as from death and / or disability.

When Social Security was initially created back in 1935 by President Franklin Roosevelt, it was considered to be one of the best systems available to provide income to retirees, as well as certain types of financial support for the disabled and the widowed. As such, it pays out billions of dollars every year to its recipients.

The majority of those who work in paid employment and self-employment, and who pay taxes into the system, are covered by the Social Security program. Those who are generally not covered by Social Security include certain state and local government workers, along with federal employees who work in the Civil Service Retirement System.

Yet, regardless of the safety net that is provided by Social Security, this program was never intended to replace 100% of one's pre-retirement earnings. As mentioned previously, it is estimated that the income that is received from Social Security's retirement benefits really only replaces about 40% of an average wage earner's income after they retire.[1]

In addition to that, the Social Security program has also run into some funding issues throughout the years. This system is financed primarily through payroll taxes that are charged on workers' earnings. On top of taxes on earnings, there are also two additional funding sources for Social Security - these include interest from the Social Security Trust Fund assets, and the taxation of Social Security benefits themselves.

Throughout the years, though, there has been a substantial strain placed on these assets. There are a couple of reasons for this. One is the sheer number of people who are becoming eligible to receive Social Security retirement benefits.

With the aging of the Baby Boomer population - those who were born between 1946 and 1964 - more and more people are retiring every year, and in turn, are claiming their benefits from Social Security. In fact, it has been estimated that starting on January 1st, 2011, and for the next 19 years, approximately 10,000 Baby Boomers will be turning 65 every single day in the United States.[2] This is compounded even further by our longer life expectancies. Today, people are living longer than ever before. Back in 1935, when Social Security was initially put into place, the average life expectancy was only 61 years old.[3] Because of that, retirement benefits were paid out for a much shorter period of time. Today, however, life expectancy has increased a great deal to where many individuals and couples can reasonably expect to spend 20 or more years in retirement.

In order to help ease some of the strain on Social Security, some changes have been put into place. One of the biggest of these has been the change in what is considered to be one's "full retirement age." For many years, this was age 65 for all retirees. However, a person's full retirement age can now be as high as age 67, depending on the year of his or her birth.

Social Security Full Retirement Age

Year of Birth	Minimum Retirement Age for Full Benefits
1937 or Before	65
1938	65 + 2 months
1939	65 + 4 months
1940	65 + 6 months
1941	65 + 8 months
1942	65 + 10 months
1943 to 1954	66
1955	66 + 2 months
1956	66 + 4 months
1957	66 + 6 months
1958	66 + 8 months
1959	66 + 10 months
1960 or Later	67

Source: SSA Publication 05-10024, Aug. 2011

Given that Social Security may only replace a small portion of your pre-retirement earnings, coupled with this program's uncertain long-term future, it is important to have other fuel available in terms of a retirement income stream.

Traditional Income Source – Pensions

Another source for retirement that has been relied upon in the past is the defined benefit pension plan. Many companies have used these plans as their retirement plan of choice throughout the years.

As the name suggests, a defined benefit plan will pay out a set amount of income benefit to its recipient. The amount of that benefit is determined by a formula that takes into account the employee's salary history, as well as his or her length of employment.

For those who participated in a defined benefit pension plan, the employer would promise to pay out a specific, guaranteed amount of retirement income for the rest of their lives - and because of this, the liability of the pension income rested completely with the employer. In fact, often, all of the contribution was also made by the employer and not by the employee.

Unfortunately, due to the substantial expense of this type of plan, many employers today have stopped using defined benefit pension plans. They have in large part been replaced by defined contribution retirement plans - the most popular of which is the 401(k) plan.

Tax-Deferred Vehicles That Depend on You
In a defined contribution plan such as the 401(k), the funds that are contributed will usually come from the employee through salary deferrals, as well as possibly from a percentage of an employer matching contribution.

One of the key advantages here is that, because the contributions are tax deferred, the employee will not have to pay taxes on the amount of salary that they contribute into the 401(k) plan. Likewise, any of the investment gain within the account is also tax-deferred until the time that it is withdrawn. This can help the funds to grow and compound exponentially over time, as it is basically allowing for gains on top of non-taxed gains each year. For the most part, though, it is solely up to the employee to ensure that he or she has enough money in the account at retirement time to convert over to an ongoing income stream. Therefore, there are no guarantees with these types of accounts like there are with the defined benefit pension plan.
There is also a maximum amount of contribution that an employee may defer into his or her 401(k) plan each year. For 2015 and 2016, that amount is $18,000 if the individual is age 49 or younger, with an additional $6,000 in "catch-up" contribution allowed for those who are age 50 and above.

There are also potential penalties to look out for with 401(k) plans. For example, a penalty could be incurred if a 401(k) plan participant withdraws funds "early," meaning that the employee withdraws money prior to turning age 59 1/2 - other than for one of the few IRS-allowed exceptions. Funds that are taken out prior to this time will be imposed a penalty of 10% of the total amount of the money that is withdrawn.

Conversely, once an individual reaches the age of 70 1/2, they will be required to start taking at least a minimum amount of withdrawals from their 401(k) plan, if they have not already started doing so. This is known as a Required Minimum Distribution, or RMD.

One of the primary advantages of the 401(k) plan is that they allow a high level of salary deferral by employee participants. In addition, due to the tax-deferral of the funds within the account, a higher potential for growth is allowed over time. Yet, even with all of these advantages of investing through a 401(k), there is still the drawback in that the employee is not truly in control of their funds until the time that they reach retirement. In addition, there is no control over which options will be available for investment in the plan. Here, the employer will typically allow various choices such as mutual funds, and possibly other options such as the employer's own stock shares (if applicable), money market funds, and a cash account.

For those who are nearing retirement, as well as those who may have maxed out other qualified retirement savings options, there are also some additional alternatives available that allow for tax-deferred growth of funds, along with a way to provide an income stream in the future.

One of these is the annuity. Although there are certainly both pros and cons to placing your funds into these financial vehicles, annuities do allow for tax-deferred growth on your principal, and, provided that the lifetime income option is chosen for the distribution phase, they can also provide you with a guaranteed income for the remainder of your life - regardless of how long that may be.

Over the past several years, certain types of life insurance policies have also come into the forefront as potential vehicles for tax-deferred retirement savings, as well as a potential supplement to retirement income in the future. One such option is indexed universal life (IUL).

This permanent form of life insurance provides both a death benefit and a cash value component whereby the funds in the cash portion of the policy are allowed to take part in the movement of an underlying market index such as the S&P 500. At the same time, however, the funds are also protected from any downward market movements - so your principal is protected. As with other types of permanent life insurance, the cash in the cash value component is allowed to grow on a tax-deferred basis. And, because of the tax-free loan feature, policy holders can also opt to supplement their retirement income with these funds if they need to.

Unlike a 401(k) plan or a Traditional IRA account, there is no Required Minimum Distribution requirement, though, so the policy holder can also continue to let the funds remain in the account, growing on a tax-deferred basis past the age of 70 1/2 if he or she chooses to do so.

IRAs - Traditional and Roth
A Traditional and Roth IRAs (Individual Retirement Account) can also provide some tax-related advantages for investors. Although both of these accounts are IRAs - and both have some similarities - there are some vast differences between the two types of accounts, too.

With the Traditional IRA, most investors can save money on a pre-tax basis. Depending on the person's income level and tax filing status, they may also be able to deduct some or all of their Traditional IRA contribution from their annual income.
For example, in 2015, a single individual who earns $61,000 per year or less, can deduct 100% of their Traditional IRA

contribution. Single individuals who earn between $61,000 and $71,000 per year can deduct a portion of what they contribute to this type of IRA account.

Those Traditional IRA investors who are married and file their taxes jointly, and who earn $98,000 per year or less can deduct 100% of their Traditional IRA contribution, and those who are married and file jointly and who earn between $98,000 and $118,000 can deduct a portion of their contribution.

If you have a Roth IRA, your contributions into the account are deposited with after-tax dollars - so there is no tax deduction for your contributions here. However, the growth on your funds inside of a Roth IRA, as well as your withdrawals, are tax-free. Due to their tax advantaged status, there are some limits on the amount that an investor may contribute each year to a Traditional and a Roth IRA. For 2015, the maximum contribution amount is $5,500 for those who are age 49 and under. However, investors who are age 50 and over are allowed to make an additional $1,000 "catch-up" contribution. For 2016, these maximum IRA contribution amounts are the same.

Similar to with a 401(k) plan, those who own a Traditional IRA account are required to start making at least some minimum amount of withdrawal (a Required Minimum Distribution) when they reach age 70 1/2. This RMD requirement is not set forth, however, on a Roth IRA account.

Other Retirement Savings Vehicles

Depending on your employer and / or your employment status, there are other types of retirement plans that you may be involved in - most of which have some type of tax related advantages as well. Some of these include the following:

SEP IRA Plan

A Simplified Employee Pension, or SEP, is a type of retirement plan that may be set up by a small business. These plans are a variation of the Individual Retirement Account, or IRA. They may be set up to provide benefits for both the employer, as well as the employees of a company.

When offering a SEP IRA, the employer is required to offer participation in the plan to employees who meet all of the following criteria:

- Age 21 or over;
- Employed by the company for at least 3 of the past 5 years;
- Has earned at least $600 in compensation from the employer (in 2015).

One primary feature of the SEP IRA plan is that the contributions are 100% vested by the employer. In fact, with these types of retirement accounts, employee contributions are not allowed.

Similar to with individual IRA accounts, the funds that are in a SEP plan are allowed to grow on a tax-deferred basis. Likewise, there will be a 10% IRS "early withdrawal" penalty if funds are taken out of the account prior to the account holder turning age 59 1/2.

SIMPLE IRA Plan

A SIMPLE IRA plan is a type of salary reduction plan that allows a qualifying small businesses to offer their employees a way to save for retirement. The term SIMPLE stands for Savings Incentive Match Plans for Employees. These plans may be offered by employers that have no more than 100 employees. With a SIMPLE IRA, both the employee and the employer can make contributions into the plan - and, the employer is allowed to match the employee's contribution up to 100% of the first 3% of compensation that is deposited by the employee.

The employee's contributions to a SIMPLE IRA go in on a pre-tax basis, and, like a 401(k) plan, the earnings on the funds that are inside of the account are allowed to grow tax-deferred. Upon withdrawal, the funds will be taxed at the account holder's then-current income tax rate.

Also similar to other qualified plans, there is a 10% early withdrawal penalty on funds that are taken out prior to the employee reaching the age of 59 1/2. However, if an employee who is under age 59 1/2 has not yet participated in the plan for at least two years withdraws money from his or her SIMPLE IRA, the penalty will jump to 25% of the amount that is withdrawn.

One of the key advantages to having a SIMPLE IRA is that is allows salary reduction for the employees with very minimal administrative paperwork on the part of the employer. These plans can also allow the employee participants to contribute the amount of their choice - up to the annual maximum. In 2015, that amount is $12,500 for those who are age 49 and younger, and $15,500 for participants who are age 50 and over.

SARSEP Plan

A SARSEP is another type of retirement plan that is used by small businesses. SARSEP stands for Salary Reduction Simplified Employee Pension Plan. These plans allow employees to contribute to a SEP account with pre-tax funds, and also to reduce their net income in the year of the contribution. These plans are used by employers that have 25 or fewer employees.

While a law change prohibited new SARSEP plans from being established after 1996, companies that established these plans prior to that time are allowed to continue maintaining them for their employees who are participants in them.

In order to be eligible to participate in a SARSEP, an employee must meet all of the following criteria:

- Age 21 or older;
- Worked for the employer for at least 3 of the past 5 years;
- Earned at least $600 (in 2015) in compensation from the employer.

There are some employers that may be excluded from a SARSEP plan. These may include employers that are covered by a union agreement and whose benefits have been bargained for by the employees' union, as well as by the employer.

The Bottom Line on Retirement Plans

The retirement plan that you participate in will certainly depend on what is offered by your employer. However, regardless of whether or not your employer offers a sponsored plan, there are other options available to you such as the IRA that can typically be set up through your local bank or brokerage company. In fact today, these types of accounts can even be set up via many online sources so that you can have your money working for you in a tax-advantaged manner very quickly.

The journey towards retirement and financial independence will more than likely include a few speed bumps - one of which is taxes. Yet, while we're all familiar with the taxes that we pay throughout our lives, in some cases, there could also be a big tax bill due upon death. This is what is known as an estate tax. The IRS defines estate taxes as being "a tax on your right to transfer property at your death. It consists of an accounting of everything that you own or have certain interests in at your death. The includable property may consist of cash and securities, real estate, insurance, trusts, annuities, business interests and other assets."[1]

Although most simple estates typically don't require the filing of an estate tax return, these returns are required for estates that have combined gross assets - which include prior taxable gifts - that exceed a certain amount. For 2015, that amount is $5.43 million.[2] The federal estate tax rate on estates that exceed this amount is 40% - which can reduce one's estate significantly unless prior planning has been done.

But even for those who don't consider themselves to be wealthy, planning ahead financially can make all the difference in the world in terms of how - and how well - you live in the future. So, when it comes to basic estate planning techniques, there are a few documents that everyone should have, regardless of how much you have accumulated.

The first item on your list should be a will. Although many people don't like to think about planning for when they are gone, having a will is an essential part of your overall financial planning process. This is especially the case if you have children.

A will is actually defined as being a "legally enforceable declaration of how an individual wants his or her assets to be distributed upon their death." Within a will, a person may also state whom they wish to act as the guardian for their minor children.

When a person dies without having a valid will, they are said to have died "intestate." When this occurs, the resulting probate proceeding is often referred as an "intestacy proceeding" because the state laws will usually be applied to any asset that is owned by the individual at death that is not held in will substitute form. Without having a will, the distribution of your property and assets could be left up to the government - and in some cases, assets could even end up becoming property of the state. With that in mind, if you don't create a will, your state will essentially create one for you - and it probably won't distribute your assets in the way that you want them to be distributed.

Given our longer life expectancies now, it is important to also plan ahead just in case of incapacity. From this angle, there are certain documents that should be put into place. For example, a living will describes and instructs how an individual would or would not wish his or her end-of-life care to be managed.

A living will is a type of advance directive that takes effect when an individual is considered to be terminally ill. Advance directives are written instructions regarding future medical care about decisions that another person can make for you if you are unable to communicate such decisions yourself.

You may also consider setting up a power of attorney for your finances. This gives a designated person the authority to make legal and financial decisions for you if you are unable to do so on your own.

Because all situations are different, though, it will be important to consult an attorney to help you in setting up any type of legal arrangement such as a power of attorney, medical directive, and possibly even your will.

In any case, it will be important to get these documents in place, as well as certain types of insurance coverage that can help you to protect the money you've saved. This is because if you don't protect your savings, even the largest of portfolios can come tumbling down in the face of certain "disasters." One of those "disasters" can include the need for long-term care.

Insurance - Long-Term Care

Due in large part to our longer life expectancies today, the need for long-term care has increased significantly over the past few decades. In fact, it is estimated that once a person reaches the age of 65, there is a 70% chance that they will require long-term care at some point in their life.[3] Along with this increased need for care, the cost has also gone up.

According to Genworth's 2014 Cost of Care Survey, the national median daily rate of a private room in a skilled nursing home facility (in 2014) was $240. That equates to over $87,000 per year. But that's just an average. In some areas of the U.S., the cost is well over six figures.

Even home health care can be expensive, with a national average hourly rate of $19 for homemaker services, and $20 per hour for home health aide services (in 2014).[4] So, regardless of the type of care that someone needs, the cost can really add up. Unfortunately, many people are under the misconception that Medicare or their regular health insurance will pay for all - or at least a majority - of their long-term care expenses. This, however, is not the case.

While regular health insurance will typically pay for hospitalization and doctor visits, it will not pay for services such as care in a nursing home - especially if it is custodial care, which is the type of care that deals with assisting someone with basic needs like bathing, dressing, and eating.

Likewise, Medicare will also not pay for a majority of a person's long-term care expenses - and the costs that it will pay for, a person needs to meet all of the following criteria in order to qualify:

- Require daily skilled care, which as a practical matter, can only be provided in a skilled nursing home facility on an inpatient basis;
- Be in the hospital for at least three consecutive days - not including the day of discharge - prior to entering into a skilled nursing facility that is certified by Medicare;
- Be admitted to the skilled nursing home facility for the same condition for which he or she was treated in the hospital;
- Generally, be admitted to the skilled nursing home facility within 30 days of their discharge from the hospital; and
- Be certified by a medical professional as needing skilled nursing or skilled rehabilitation services on a daily basis.[5]

Provided that a person does meet all of the above qualification to receive Medicare benefits for skilled nursing home care, their benefits would be paid as follows:

- All approved charges for the first 20 days are fully paid for by Medicare;
- After the 20th day, the patient is responsible for a daily co-payment between days 21 and 100. In 2015, the amount of this copayment is $157.50 per day;
- If the patient requires more than 100 days of care in the skilled nursing home facility per benefit period, then he or she will be responsible for paying the entire amount that is due for their care beginning on the 101st day.[6]

So, when looking at the figures here, even if an individual does qualify for Medicare's skilled nursing home benefits, if he or she needs 100 days of care or more - which is really only a little more than three months - they would still have an out-of-pocket co-payment charge of $12,600. ($157.50 daily co-payment X 80 days) It is also important to keep in mind that Medicare's benefits only pay for skilled care. It pays nothing for intermediate or custodial care - which account for the majority of the long-term care services that most people really require.

Medicare may pay for some very limited home care services. Here again, if the patient only needs assistance with basic daily living activities such as dressing or bathing, then Medicare will not cover the cost of providing only this type of care. However, Medicare may cover the costs of medical care in the home - including help with basic activities of daily living, if this is part of a doctor's orders.[7]

Another government program, Medicaid, will actually pay for long-term care services - however there's a big caveat here in that in order for a person to qualify, they need to be considered at the poverty level.

Unfortunately, those who rely on Medicaid for their long-term care expenses will typically have far fewer choices regarding the type of care that they receive, as well as the location of where their care is received than those who pay for their care out-of-pocket or privately via a long-term care insurance policy.

In addition, while most nursing homes do accept Medicaid as a source of payment, the government allows them to set limits on the number of Medicaid patients that they can receive. So, if a nursing home has already met its Medicaid "quota," then it can essentially close its doors to any new patients who plan to pay in this way for their care.

In order to pay for long-term care, then, and still have the most choice possible, it really comes down to just a few viable ways of approaching this particular risk. These include the following:

- Self-insuring;
- Transferring all of the risk to an insurance company by purchasing a comprehensive long-term care insurance policy; or
- Sharing the risk with an insurance company.

Unfortunately, self-insuring isn't an option for many people. This is due to the sheer cost of long-term care. Given the average price tag on the cost of care in a facility, as well as the cost to have someone come into your home, it doesn't take long for an individual or a couple to quickly deplete their savings - savings that were likely earmarked for other purposes such as retirement income. And, while some individuals may still opt to "take their chances" and self-fund if the need for care arises, neither self-funding, nor obtaining government assistance, can offer all three of the following advantages that can be provided through the purchase of long-term care insurance:

- **High quality of care.** Unlike in the past, today there are numerous options for receiving high quality long-term care. Many of today's facilities include a long list of amenities, such as swimming pools, beauty salons, and regular social events for their residents - oftentimes resembling country clubs rather than long-term care facilities. Most long-term care insurance policies today will also offer the option to receive care at home - which is where most people would prefer to be.

- **Protection of assets.** In addition to paying for the care that is needed, long-term care insurance can help policy holders to keep their own assets safe and in-tact so that these funds can be used for their originally intended purpose. This can be especially beneficial for married couples where one spouse is still healthy and needs assets and / or income in order to continue maintaining a home and other living expenses.

- **Tax advantages.** On top of all the other benefits that long-term care insurance can provide, there may also be certain tax incentives available for purchasing this type of coverage. Today, most of the long-term care insurance policies that are sold are tax-qualified, meaning that the premiums on these policies could qualify as being an itemized tax deduction - up to a certain amount for a taxpayer. Depending on a policy holder's age and other medical expenses that they incur, he or she may be able to deduct a certain portion of the long-term care insurance premium that they pay each year - making the coverage even more affordable. As an example, if an individual is age 64 or younger during the 2015 tax year, what they pay in long-term care insurance premium may be deductible, as long as the amount exceeds 10% of his or her adjusted gross income. If a policy holder is age 65 or older, this threshold is 7.5% of their adjusted gross income - through the tax year 2016.

The amount of long-term care insurance premium that may be deducted is limited to a certain dollar amount that is dependent on the policy holder's age. In 2015, the deductible limits for eligible tax-qualified long-term care insurance premiums that are includable as a medical expense are as follows:

Attained Age Before Close of Taxable Year	2015
40 or under	$380
More than 40 but not more than 50	$710
More than 50 but not more than 60	$1,430
More than 60 but not more than 70	$3,800
Over 70	$4,750

Source: IRS Revenue Procedure 2014-61

Most long-term care insurance policies that are issued today will provide coverage for a wide variety of benefits, including:

- Skilled nursing home facility
- Assisted living facility
- Home care

Policies may also include additional coverage for benefits such as adult day care, hospice care, and / or respite care so that a family member or other loved one who is caring for the insured may take a break.

When applying for coverage, an applicant can typically choose how long they want the benefits paid out, such as 2 years, 3 years, or 5 years. In the past, many insurance carriers offered an unlimited or lifetime benefit option, however, some insurers have scaled back on this particular option due to the expense.

Applicants can usually choose to add an inflation rider to their policy benefits in order to keep the benefit payout on pace with the rising cost of care over time.

Just as with other types of insurance, long-term care will usually require a type of deductible before the coverage will begin. In this case, the deductible comes in the form of a waiting period, or elimination period.

The elimination period is the time period after the onset of a loss - such as entering a skilled nursing home or the need for home health care - during which benefits are not paid. Once the elimination period has been met, however, the policy will begin to pay for covered services.

There are a number of different variables that will determine how much a long-term care insurance policy will cost. These typically include the:

- Age of the insured
- Dollar amount of benefits to be paid
- Inflation rider chosen
- Elimination period
- Duration of benefits

Policy holders may also be able to qualify for a premium discount on their coverage. For instance, if an individual is in exceptionally good health at the time of application, they may be able to obtain a preferred health discount. Also, many insurance companies will offer a spousal or partner discount to couples if both spouses or partners apply for long-term care insurance at the same time.

Required Minimum Distributions

As investors reach a certain age, there are various retirement accounts that may require at least a minimum amount of withdrawal to be made each year. This Required Minimum Distribution, or RMD, is what the federal government mandates is taken out of retirement accounts such as Traditional IRAs, SIMPLE

IRAs, SEP IRAs, and many employer-sponsored plans such as 401(k)s, when a person reaches age 70 1/2.

An individual is required to take his or her first required RMD for the year in which they turn age 70 1/2. However, the first actual payment is allowed to be delayed until April 1st of the year following the year in which they turn age 70 1/2. For all of the years following that - including the year in which the investor was paid the initial distribution - the individual must take the withdrawal by December 31st of that year.[8]

It is important to abide by these RMD rules. Otherwise, you stand to be penalized - and these penalties can tend to be somewhat hefty. For example, according to the IRS, if an account holder doesn't withdraw his or her RMD - or even if they just simply do not withdraw the full amount of their required withdrawal, or if they fail to make their RMD by the necessary deadline date - then the amount that has not been withdrawn will be taxed at a rate of 50%.[9]

Annuities

One way that investors can look ahead towards retirement in terms of securing a guaranteed income, while at the same time obtaining some nice tax benefits, is through the use of annuities. An annuity is actually a contract between an individual and an insurance company. This contract can guarantee a stream of income to the person whose life is based on it - otherwise known as the "annuitant" - in return for either a lump sum deposit, or for periodic deposits that are made over time. The gain that occurs inside of the annuity is tax deferred until it is either paid out as income or it is withdrawn.

Annuities can be structured in a number of different ways with regard to the manner in which they are funded, as well as with how - and for how long - they pay out funds to the annuitant. This can give annuity purchasers a great deal of flexibility in setting up the contract in order to meet their specific needs.
The types of annuities that are available in the market include:

- **Fixed Annuities** - Fixed annuities will offer their holders a fixed amount of interest that is credited on an annual basis. This rate is declared by the insurance carrier that offers the annuity. The key benefit to owning a fixed annuity is the safety of principal that it provides.

- **Variable Annuities** - Variable annuities are set up in a similar manner as fixed annuities, however, these vehicles allow their holders to participate in market appreciation via a number of different investment options. These underlying investments are typically held in "sub-accounts" and they will often include equities such as mutual funds. Those who own variable annuities have the opportunity to grow the value of the account based on market performance. They are also, however, subject to downward market risk.

- **Indexed Annuities** - An indexed annuity is a type of annuity that has its return linked to an underlying market index such as the S&P 500 or the DJIA (Dow Jones Industrial Average). The owners of an indexed annuity are not actually purchasing shares in the investment, but rather interest is credited to their account based on changes in the index to which the annuity is linked.

One appealing characteristic of an annuity is the income stream that it can provide. This is one reason why annuities are purchased by those who are retired or those who are approaching retirement. Most annuities will have the following types of income payout options available:

- **Period Certain** - The period certain income payout option will pay out a regular, recurring income for a set number of years, no matter how long the annuitant lives. Once the number of years has elapsed, there will be no more income payments from the annuity.

- **Life Only** - The life only payout option will provide the annuitant with income payments throughout the rest of his or her life - regardless of how long they may live.

- **Life with Period Certain** - This payout option is a combination of the period certain option and the life only option in that it provides payments for the rest of the annuitant's lifetime. However, if the annuitant passes away shortly after the income payments begin, a named beneficiary will still receive income from the annuity for a set number of years.

- **Joint and Survivor** - The joint and survivor payout option will provide an income to two annuitants for the remainder of both of their lives. This income choice is oftentimes used by couples to help in ensuring that each person has an income that will last throughout each of their lifetimes.

In addition to a regular, guaranteed stream of income, annuities can also offer additional benefits as well. For example, these vehicles will oftentimes provide a death benefit feature where if the annuitant passes away before receiving back all of their deposited funds, a lump sum of cash will be paid to a named beneficiary.

Some annuities will also include a long-term care or nursing home rider in the contract that allows the annuitant to receive funds from the contract if they should require certain types of care.

The Bottom Line

While saving for retirement is important, ensuring that savings are protected from bumps along the road such as estate taxes and / or a potential long-term care need is also an essential part of planning for the journey. Placing these additional coordinates into your GPS now will be another key part of making sure that you arrive safely at your ultimate destination.

Sources
1. www.IRS.gov (https://www.irs.gov/Businesses/Small-Businesses-&-Self-Employed/Estate-Tax)
2. Ibid
3. http://www.longtermcare.gov
4. Genworth 2014 Cost of Care Survey. Genworth. (https://www.genworth.com/dam/Americas/US/PDFs/Consumer/corporate/130568_032514_CostofCare_FINAL_nonsecure.pdf)
5. http://www.medicare.gov
6. Ibid
7. Ibid
8. www.IRS.gov (https://www.irs.gov/Retirement-Plans/Retirement-Plans-FAQs-regarding-Required-Minimum-Distributions)
9. Ibid

Sources

1. SSA - Social Security - Understanding the Benefits. Page 4. (http://www.socialsecurity.gov/pubs/EN-05-10024.pdf)

2. Baby Boomers Retire. Pew Research Center. December 29, 2010. (http://www.pewresearch.org/daily-number/baby-boomers-retire/)

3. The Social Security Dilemma. EDGE. (https://web.stanford.edu/class/e297c/poverty_prejudice/soc_sec/hsocialsec.htm)

Chapter Seven: Your Home

One of the biggest investments that most people will ever make in their lifetime is their home. So, once your GPS has taken you closer to retirement, one of the key questions you must ask yourself is what you intend to do with that investment going forward.

In the past, most retirees would have long paid off their mortgage balance. But that is not necessarily so in today's world. Many of today's retirees may also be residing with adult children - or possibly even grandchildren. So, there are a myriad of decisions that will often have to be made when it comes to whether or not to keep the family home - and if not, where will you end up living?

Will You Stay in Your Home?

Upon retiring from the world of work, one of the questions you'll need to ask yourself is whether or not you will remain in your present home. For some, the answer may come easy, as friends and family may all be within close proximity and the thought of leaving would actually be more of a detriment. For others, though, getting out on the open road may be something that you've been looking forward to for many years.
When determining whether or not you will stay in your home, there are a number of factors that will be important to consider. These will typically include the following:

Lifestyle and Amenities

Where you choose to live in retirement can depend in large part upon the lifestyle that you choose to live. Many people work all their lives dreaming about how they will spend their time playing golf, hiking, or walking on the beach, once their employment days are over. So, with that in mind, depending on whether or not you have a specific place or geographic area already decided upon, you will need to consider where you want to reside.

If you haven't decided where your route will take you, ask yourself some questions, such as:

- How will you spend your days?
- What activities do you intend to do in retirement?
- What type of weather do you prefer?

Proximity to Family

For many people, being close to family and loved ones can also be an important consideration in retirement - whether that means remaining in an area where your family already lives, or moving to an area in order to be close to loved ones.

In some cases, it could also mean leaving your home for long periods of time in order to travel to different areas and visit with loved ones, now that you have the time available to do so. In this instance, it often makes sense to "downsize" to a smaller home or condo that is easier to leave for long stretches of time without having to worry about a lot of upkeep.

Aging

Certainly, aging will also be a primary concern when it comes to keeping your home or moving on to other alternatives. For those retirees who are in the younger age brackets - or who are in relatively good health - remaining in your home may be a potential option.

For others, however, aging or health related issues may force you to consider alternate living arrangements. This can especially be the case if you live in a home that has many steps to contend with and / or is not compatible in other ways for your current or future physical needs.

Tapping the Value of Your Home

If you do decide to keep your home - and if you have a great deal of equity in the property - you could possibly tap into it as an additional source of retirement income. There are several ways of doing this, such as by refinancing, taking a home equity loan, or obtaining a reverse mortgage.

If you opt to refinance your home, you could pull cash from the property's value by taking out a larger mortgage. Even though you would still have a mortgage payment to make, you would also have a lump sum of cash from the refinance that could subsequently be converted into a stream of retirement income either via systematic withdrawals, annuitization, or the purchase of income producing bonds and / or dividend paying stocks. A home equity loan could also work in a similar fashion, allowing you to use the proceeds from the home's refinance or home equity loan to place into an annuity or to set up a systematic withdrawal plan.

It is important here, however, to determine whether the interest rate on the home equity loan will "erase" a percentage of income gain on the annuity or your systematic withdrawal rate. In addition, because a home equity loan will also increase your debt, you will need to be mindful of how the repayment amount will affect your overall income to expense ratio.

In the case of either a refinance or taking out a home equity loan, the payments that are made towards these loans would consist of both principal and interest. The portion that is interest could be deducted on your annual tax return.

A reverse mortgage may offer you another way to convert home equity into a stream of income. Reverse mortgages are loans against the equity in your home that can provide you with a cash advance, yet they require no mandatory monthly repayments during the life of the loan.

If the interest is unpaid, it is allowed to accrue against the value of the home. In addition, if you choose to pay even a portion of the interest, it could be deductible against the value of the home. With a reverse mortgage, a loan or a line of credit is secured by a homeowner that is based upon the value of the home, as well as the amount of equity that you have in the property. Other factors include your age - you must be at least 62 years old - as well as current interest rates. Typically, the older you are and the more equity you have in your home, the more money that can be secured by a reverse mortgage.

Methods of securing funds from a reverse mortgage include a line of credit, a regular income payment, or a single lump sum of cash. Reverse mortages do not need to be repaid until the homeowner passes away, sells the home, or permanently moves out of the property.

Chapter Eight: Your Retirement Roadmap

As you design your retirement roadmap, you may find that there are a myriad of detours and side streets that can take you off your course. There are also many possible opportunities to either slow down or speed up your progress. That's why it's important to stay focused on your ultimate destination.

Building a Balanced Portfolio

One of the best ways to do so is to build a balanced investment portfolio. While you may hear stories about "hitting it big" or striking it rich with just one or two "hot" stocks, the truth is that real wealth is made by building a solid foundation and then growing your funds from there.

In order to build a successful balanced portfolio, you will need to plug in a couple of key values to your GPS device. These will include your investing time horizon, your preferred investment style(s), and your tolerance for risk. Knowing all of these factors will help in guiding you as you make your way through the journey.

Time Horizon

First, your investment time horizon can be defined in a couple of ways. Overall, it is the length of time between now and the time that you wish to retire. For some people, this may be many years. For others, it could be only a few.

Each of the individual investments that you purchase will also have its own time horizon. For example, when going into a particular investment, you should have at least some idea of how long you will keep that financial vehicle. This is oftentimes determined based upon your overall objectives, your growth and/or income needs, as well as your tolerance for risk.

Investment Styles

When riding on the road to retirement, you will typically run across several different styles of investing. These are generally categorized based in large part on the amount of riskiness that the underlying investments tend to take on - and, depending on your time horizon, as well as your risk tolerance, the type of investments that you choose to put into your portfolio will often be influenced by the particular category that an investment falls into.

The primary investment styles include:

Growth

Growth investors typically have a goal of producing a high return from their invested funds. Many of the vehicles that may be chosen in this category may have a higher price volatility than those that are in the income or growth and income category. Examples may include individual growth stocks, growth mutual funds, growth stock unit trusts, and growth variable annuities. These investments will oftentimes pay little or no current dividends as well.

Income

Income investors may take on a small amount of risk, however, they also are seeking vehicles that will produce cash flow in return for their invested funds. In other words, these investors are seeking yield.

Additional characteristics may include fixed interest or dividend payments. Typically, the market value of income investments will change in the opposite direction of changes in interest rates. Income investments can include bonds, bond mutual funds, CDs, and preferred stock.

Growth and Income

Growth and income investors take on somewhat more risk than income only investors in exchange for obtaining both current income, along with the opportunity for their principal to grow faster than the rate of inflation. With growth and income investments, dividend payments from a stock investment could possibly also increase over time as well.

Some examples of growth and income investments may include utility stocks, blue chip stocks, stock unit investment trusts, growth and income mutual funds, balanced mutual funds, convertible bonds, and real estate investment trusts (REITS).

Value

Value investing is defined as selecting stocks that trade for less than their intrinsic values. Those who are value investors, then, will seek out stocks of companies that they feel are undervalued in the market.

In the case of value investing, an investor may believe that the market over-reacts to bad and good news - and as a result, the movement of certain stock prices do not actually move or correspond with the companies true long-term fundamentals. Because of this, the investor feels that there is a good opportunity to profit by purchasing the shares the underlying company stock when the price is deflated.

Risk Tolerance

Another extremely important element in ensuring that you don't run off the road is knowing what your risk tolerance is - and then investing within those parameters. In other words, investors should have a realistic understanding of their ability to stomach large swings in the value of their investments. This is because those who take on too much risk in their investing may tend to panic - which could in turn cause them to sell their investments at the wrong time. This could result in unnecessary - and costly - losses.

With that in mind, you should always go into every investment knowing what your true risk tolerance is - and if you are not comfortable with a particular investment, then you should forgo it and move on to something else that will allow you to sleep at night as you continue down the road to retirement.

Chapter Nine: Risks

As with most any type of journey, there will be risks along the route as you make your way towards retirement. If you are unaware of these risks, or if you haven't properly prepared for them, they could throw you off course, leading you down a path that you really didn't want to go.

But, for those who anticipate these potential risks up front - and even going so far as to put possible "detours" into their GPS tracking device - these bumps along the road will seem like a perfectly normal part of the trip.

Market Risk

One of the biggest risk that you could face is market risk. The constant ups and downs of the stock market means that you will need to protect what you have saved - because even a slight market "correction" could essentially wipe out years of what you have worked for.

Protection of principal is something that many investors aim for - this is especially fresh in the minds of anyone who may have lost money in the market downturn of 2008. Even today, the market can have substantial short-term swings - and making up for a drop in asset value isn't always easy.

For instance, if a stock drops by 50% of its value, it will actually need to rise by 100% just to get back to even again. As an example, if the price of a stock starts out at $10 per share, and it drops by 50%, then the price will go to $5. If the price then rises by 50%, it will only be at $7.50. Therefore, in order to get back to its original starting point of $10 per share, the stock would actually need to gain 100% - which is twice as much as it originally dropped.

With that in mind, investors have to find a way to protect themselves from too much market risk - while at the same time, keeping an ample amount of money invested in equities in order to keep up with future inflation. A well-diversified portfolio can help to get you there.

Inflation Risk

Inflation is another key risk to your retirement funds - and over time, it can also play a role in affecting your retirement income as well. One reason for this is because people are living so much longer today and are needing their income to last for a much longer period of time.

Think about how much the price of our basic necessities has risen over just the past ten years - for instance, food, gas, and utilities. All of these things will still be necessary for you to purchase - even after you stop earning a paycheck from your employer. So, you will need to ensure that you not only have a long-term stream of income coming in, but also that your income will continue rising over time to keep up with increasing prices.

If, as an example, the average inflation rate is just over 3%, it can essentially cut your purchasing power by one-half in just a 20-year period of time. This means if you retired today, your income would have to double in 20 years just to purchase the same goods and services that you purchase now. So, if your investments were earning you $4,000 per month right now, they would have to earn $8,000 per month 20 years down the road just to keep pace with inflation.

Interest Rate Risk

Interest rate risk can also have an effect on your investments, as well as your long-term income. This is the risk that the value of an investment will change due to the level of interest rates. It can be especially worrisome to those who are holding bonds in that the value of the bond may rise or fall based on an interest rate change after the investor purchases the bond. But interest rate risk can also affect securities.

As an example, a bond paying 5% will be worth more if interest rates fall. This is because the holder of the bond is receiving a fixed rate of interest in relation to the market - which is offering a lower rate of return as a result of the decrease in interest rates. If interest rates rise, the bond will be worth less because it pays less than prevailing market rates.

Here again, one of the best ways of reducing this type of risk is to have a well-diversified portfolio. For someone who is already retired, this could mean investing in fixed income vehicles that all possess different durations.

Changes in interest can be risky in other ways, too. For instance, they can impact the cost of borrowing money, as well as one's ability to obtain - or not obtain - credit. For instance, when interest rates rise, it can make borrowing money much more expensive. That means that getting a mortgage, a car loan, or any other type of loan will be much more costly to pay back.

Even the difference between one-half or one percent interest can make a substantial difference in the total amount that a borrower repays over time. When rates become too high, they could even prevent some borrowers - primarily those with lower credit scores - from being able to obtain loans at all.

Global Turmoil

Today, many investors don't just place their funds into U.S. based financial vehicles. By branching out internationally, investors can significantly increase their diversification opportunities - along with the potential return on their portfolios. One reason for this is because the stock prices of international companies can go up and down at different times than U.S. companies - which may actually reduce the overall volatility of one's portfolio.

However, with some of these advantages can also come some risk - one of which is global turmoil. It can be difficult at best for investors to guard against unexpected revolutions, interest rate movements, and even general unrest in foreign countries. Therefore, it will be essential to not put "all of your eggs into one basket" when investing in overseas assets.

Asset Classes and Allocation

It is also important to stay well diversified among different asset classes. There are numerous different types of asset classes, just as there are many different roads that can take you to a certain destination.

Depending on your mode of transportation, the amount of time that you have (or want) to spend getting there, and the amount of risk that you're comfortable with taking, you will need to factor all of that into the route that you choose to take.

Imagine sitting down and looking at a giant map. You are in one spot right now, and you want to get to another - a place called retirement - in the future. There are numerous different ways in which you can get there - and the vehicles below could all play a part in how you do.

Some of the vehicles you have to choose from include:

Stocks

When you invest in stocks, you have the opportunity to increase your wealth a great deal. However, before moving forward, it is important to understand exactly what you are investing in, and how the process works.

First, when you own a share of stock, you are basically becoming a part owner of the underlying company - and, it is that ownership structure that gives a stock its value. Typically, the price of a stock will track the earnings of that underlying company. Therefore, a good stock may rise in price - even if the stock market as a whole is going down on a particular day, and vice versa. The price of a stock may also be based on projections of the company's future earnings.

Throughout the years, stocks have been considered to be very solid investments, for the most part. As our economy has grown, so have corporate earnings - as well as the prices of many companies' stocks.

Even though, on average, stocks have returned approximately 10% over time, the term "over time" can be relative - and, with the volatility of the stock market, the return on individual shares can also be unsettled.

In the short term time frame, the behavior of the stock market can often be based more on news, the media, and even sometimes on fear. Over the longer term, though, it is primarily company earnings that can determine whether the price of a stock will go up or down - or sideways.

Regardless of what the current market conditions are, investing in stocks should typically be considered as a long term endeavor. In most cases, it is smarter to buy and hold the shares of good, solid companies than it is to engage in short-term trading.

Investors who have a longer time horizon may be able to invest more heavily in stocks. However, for those with a shorter time horizon and who are approaching retirement, good solid dividend-paying stocks could be a good option. Investing for the long term in stocks should include creating a portfolio that is well diversified with companies from several different industries, and possibly from different countries as well.

Bonds

Bonds can encompass a wide variety of different financial instruments - each with a varying degrees of risk and reward. Governments and businesses can issue bonds in order to fund their day to day operations or to obtain the funds that are needed for the financing of certain projects.

When you invest in a bond, you are actually lending your funds to the issuer of that bond for a certain period of time. In return for your loaned funds, you - the bond holder - will receive back your original amount of funds in the future, along with regular payments of interest from the bond issuer on a regular basis.
In most instances, the value of a bond will move in the opposite direction as interest rates. For instance, when the rate of interest falls, the price of a bond will go up. Alternatively, when interest rates rise, then the prices of bonds will go down.

If you hold on to a bond until it matures, the movements in the market will not matter so much, as you will still receive back the original amount that you paid in - plus your regular payments of interest over time.

Many retirees will invest in bonds so that they can receive a fixed retirement income from the regular interest payments. It is important, though, to still keep some growth-related vehicles such as stocks included in the portfolio so as to help keep pace with inflation. Otherwise, a retiree could fall behind on future purchasing power.

Other Asset Types

When it comes to investing, there are numerous other types of assets to choose from as well. It is important to be aware of what else is available, and how other types of investments work, so as to build a well-diversified portfolio overall.

Some of the other primary investment types include:

- **Certificates of Deposit (CD)** - Certificates of deposit are time deposits that are typically offered to investors through banks, credit unions, and investment companies. These are considered to be good, safe savings vehicles because they are insured, and virtually risk free from market fluctuations. A CD has a specific fixed term and also usually a fixed rate of interest. The interest rate on a CD is usually higher than that of a savings account. Common time frames on CDs are 3 months, 6 months, 1 year, and 5 years. It is usually intended that the owner of a CD will hold the investment until the time it matures. At that time, the money may be withdrawn, along with the interest that has been accrued. If, however, the investor cashes out of the CD early, they will typically be charged a penalty.

- **Mutual Funds** - A mutual fund is made up of a pool of money that has been collected from numerous investors. The purpose of a mutual fund is to invest in a variety of different securities, which may include stocks, bonds, money markets, and other types of assets. Mutual funds may pool money from hundreds, or even thousands, of investors in order to construct a portfolio. When an investor purchases shares in a mutual fund, they will get a stake in all of its underlying investments. A mutual fund is operated by a money manager (or a group of managers) whose job it is to invest the fund's capital in line with its stated objectives. Mutual funds are actually purchased in "units" or shares. These units are issued, and can be bought or sold at the fund's net asset value (NAV) per share. A key advantage of investing in mutual funds is that an investor can gain access to a well-diversified portfolio without having to invest a large amount of money - as some mutual funds will allow you to begin investing with as little as $100.

- **Unit Investment Trusts (UITs)** - A unit investment trust is defined as being an investment company that offers a type of fixed and "unmanaged" portfolio. The portfolio typically includes a diversified mix of different stocks and / or bonds that are selected by the UIT's manager, with the goal of meeting the UIT's stated investment objective. These underlying financial vehicles are redeemable as "units" to the investors in the unit investment trust for a set period of time. The primary goal of a UIT is to offer either dividend income and / or capital appreciation to its holders.

- **Exchange Traded Funds (ETFs)** - An Exchange Traded Fund is a type of security that tracks an index, a commodity, or even a group of assets in a similar manner as an index fund. However, an ETF will actually trade like a stock on a market exchange. These vehicles will also have regular price fluctuations throughout the trading day. Like a mutual fund, ETFs contain a "basket" of many different stocks and other financial assets that are all combined into one single investment. Also similar to a mutual fund, exchange traded funds are sold in shares via the open market to investors. Typically, the goal of an ETF is to match the return of a certain market index (or multiple market indexes).

Transaction Costs and Fees

Regardless of the financial vehicle that you are investing in, it is likely that there will be some type of a transaction cost or fee involved. Investors should consider this as a part of their "fuel" cost and factor it into the journey. That being said, however, it should also be considered when factoring in your overall return, as it can make a difference in what you "net" out of the overall investment.

Different asset classes will have varying ranges of standard transaction costs and fees. So, prior to moving forward with any type of investment, it is essential to be aware of what those costs will be.

What is Your Investor Personality Type?

Just as we all have our own unique personality type in general, investors have varying manners in how they go about investing. Some may dive in head first, full steam ahead, while others will take a more cautious approach - and in some instances, being even a bit too cautious.

Knowing your investor personality type is important because it can help you in charting your course for moving forward. It can also help you to stay on track so that you don't veer off course or get too far behind.

DIY and the Dangers of No Strategy Discipline

While going about things "your own way" and doing it yourself (DIY) may work in certain areas of life, when it comes to investing for the future, this is no place for cutting corners. And, while you may feel that you are saving money on brokerage fees and commissions, those savings could pale in comparison to what you're actually losing out on.

For example, one of the biggest mistakes that do-it-yourselfers make is not creating a proper financial plan before they invest. Therefore, moving forward without consideration for your time horizon, risk tolerance, and appropriate asset allocation can lead you down a path that takes you in a direction that has nothing to do with where you actually want to go. This can be very costly. Another big mistake that managing your finances on your own can conjure up is in the area of taxes. This can be a complex matter - and in many cases, investors may not even always realize what the tax implications are behind their investment decisions. But the reality is that just about all financial decisions have some type of taxable event associated with them - so it's better to know what that is up front.

Investors who go forward on their own may oftentimes also end up chasing performance. Unfortunately, though, this can lead to poor investment decisions, as well as some bad investment timing. This type of investing can also lead to going with financial vehicles that may have nothing at all to do with your specific financial goals.

The Benefits of Professional Management

A much better way to go about your investing is with the help of a professional financial advisor. This way, you will have someone there to help in guiding you along the entire journey. A professional advisor can help you to create the plan that will move you towards achieving your short- and long-term financial goals. And, they can also provide you with insight on what to do if and when the road gets bumpy - because we know that it undoubtedly will.

Having a plan - and a coach to ensure that you stick to it - may appear somewhat mundane at times. Yet, doing so is much more likely to be profitable than going the DIY route. This can allow you a much better opportunity to attain the goals that you have set - which in turn, will be much more rewarding to you overall.

Even with the most well planned course, you may find along your journey that there will be road construction, accidents, or any number of other unexpected events that can cause you to have to change direction - even if only slightly - in order to get you to your ultimate destination.

In some cases, this may require you to rebalance your portfolio. Rebalancing refers to realigning the weightings of the different assets that are in your portfolio in order to maintain your desired level of asset allocation. Doing so can help you to remain on course - even if the original route has changed somewhat.
So, how do you know when it may be time to sell certain assets or to make various changes?

In most cases, this will be a result of regularly reviewing your portfolio. In fact, a regular check of your financial assets - just like a regular tune up for your car - is essential in order to ensure that things are going the way they are supposed to. Otherwise, the end result could be far from what you'd anticipated.
When rebalancing your assets, it can help if you have a master list of everything that you own - not just the assets in one account such as your 401(k). That way, you will be able to better apportion the total amount of your funds across the board.

There are actually two ways in which you can then go about rebalancing your portfolio. One way - which is actually the easiest - is to simply redirect all future investment dollars into any asset classes that are under-represented. This strategy would also include ceasing to contribute to funds that are considered to be "too weighted."

The other rebalancing approach - which may be a more precise method - would be to actually buy and sell various assets until your total portfolio is in line with your desired asset allocation mix for the goals that you wish to achieve. This means selling off the asset classes that are overvalued, and likewise buying the undervalued ones.

Most financial professionals suggest that you review your portfolio at least once each year. That way, if a particular asset, or asset class, has outperformed another, you will have the chance to realign and prepare yourself going forward.
Rebalancing will also help you to maintain your original asset allocation strategy and to remain with your investment plan and goals - no matter what has occurred in the stock market - or in even in the economy as a whole.

Once you have reached your retirement date, it will be time to take what you have saved and convert it over into an income stream. For many people, it will seem strange at first switching over from an "accumulation" mode to a "decumulation" state of mind.

One reason for this is because for so many years, we are taught that we need to save our money. But retirement is the time where we can live off of what we've saved - provided that we have enough.

Making Sure You Have Enough Money

In order to ensure that you can actually leave the "security" of your employer's regular paycheck, you will need to have enough money to live on. So, prior to stepping into the world of retirement, you will need to get an idea of how much you will require to live on.

Setting up a retirement budget can help. This will entail listing all of the monthly expenses that you anticipate having once you retire. While some of these may be the same as they are prior to retirement, others will likely change.

Ideally, you should create a monthly budget that includes your mandatory expenses, such as food, housing, and utilities - in other words, the items that you have to have in order to live. Then, you should also include another list of non-essential expenses such as travel, fun, and other items that you would like to include. Once you have totaled up the amount, you will have a monthly dollar figure to shoot for.

Next, make a list of all of the potential income sources that you anticipate having in retirement. These may include Social Security, income from an employer-sponsored savings plan such as a 401(k), and additional income from personal investments. After you have an idea of your total monthly income and your total monthly expenses, you will be able to see whether or not you have enough. If so, then you are on track. If not, then you may need to find ways of filling in the income "gaps." This can oftentimes be done by either reducing your expenses, or by adding income such as working part-time. You could also opt to delay your retirement date in order to add more funds to your savings - which could in turn, help to increase the income that is generated from it.

Strategies to Make Sure You Never Outlive Your Money

Because our life expectancies are longer now, planning for a retirement of 20 or more years is common today. Therefore, it is important to know that you will not only have an ongoing income stream - but also ideally one that will increase over time so as to keep up with inflation.

Throughout the years, Social Security has usually provided an increase in its annual retirement benefits. (Although there have been some years where there was no annual cost of living increase given). This increase can help retirees to keep up with the rising cost of goods and services in the future.

When setting up your own income streams from investments, you will need to ensure that your income goes up over time, too. In some cases, financial vehicles can be set to automatically do so. For example, many annuities will offer the option of increasing the income on a regular basis to the recipient.

There are also ways to set up receipt of a certain percentage of income from your investment portfolio, while leaving the remainder in the account to continue growing. Working with a professional financial advisor can help you in creating the plan that works best for you and your specific goals.

Providing for Spouses and Other Loved Ones

If you have a spouse or other loved ones that you wish to provide for, this too will be important when setting up your retirement income plan. Depending on your goals, you could set up various alternatives.

For instance, many annuities offer the joint lifetime income option. When choosing this income payout option, each spouse or partner will receive guaranteed lifetime income throughout the remainder of their lives - regardless of how long they live. This can be an ideal way of ensuring that both individuals have income for the rest of their lives.

You can also ensure that a spouse or other loved one is protected through insurance. As an example, there are some types of retirement pension plans that will stop paying income at the death of the primary income recipient. This can be detrimental to a surviving spouse, however, who could find herself (or himself) suddenly without an income source. Therefore, by purchasing life insurance, the spouse who passes away can ensure that the death benefit proceeds will replace the lost income for their surviving spouse.

Here again, working with a financial professional can help you in finding the income and the protection plan that is the very best fit for you particular needs.

Keeping a Grip on Expenses

Another way to help in ensuring that your retirement income will last for a longer period of time is to keep a good grip on your expenses. Unlike when you were working, the amount of your retirement income pool may be limited and running short - so every dollar that you spend may need to be watched and accounted for.

Having a budget in retirement can help you to keep close track of your income and your outgo - and in turn, it can be a great way to reduce a financial stress. This can assist you in making your retirement more enjoyable overall.

Regardless of how well you have planned, sometimes even the most well mapped out course will need to be re-routed. This could be due to economic or market-related adjustments or to changes in your life that call for an alteration of your financial goals.

While changes will require you to re-route, it is important to keep in mind that this is not unusual. In fact, life is filled with all kinds of changes. The good news is that by re-coordinating your GPS system, you will be back on track, and again moving towards your destination.

Options to Increase Income

As you approach retirement - or even if you're already a retiree - there are a number of ways that you can increase your income in order to get back on track. These can include the following:

- **Working Part-Time** - Even though you may have retired from your full-time employment, there are many retirees who take on part-time work - even if it's just a temporary endeavor. In some cases, you may want to try a new and different opportunity, and in others, getting out for a few hours each day or each week can be a nice way to meet new people and be social, along with earning some additional cash.

- **Buying Dividend Producing Stocks** - Dividend producing stocks are another option for helping to increase your income. Oftentimes, these are good solid opportunities that will pay out on a regular basis. Depending on the company, and the amount of the dividend, you could tack on a nice stream of extra income.

- **Owning Rental Real Estate** - Although becoming a landlord isn't for everyone, it can be a nice source of additional income for retirees. And, it doesn't always entail having to purchase a property. If you have an extra bedroom or a finished basement, you could consider renting out that space. Likewise, if you're considering moving or downsizing, rather than selling your current home, possibly you could rent it out instead and add the monthly income stream to your incoming retirement cash flow.

- **Increasing Your Social Security Benefits** - If you have not yet begun to take your Social Security retirement benefits, there are some strategies that could help you to give yourself a "raise" with this income source, too. For example, for every year that you delay taking benefits after your full retirement age, your monthly benefit will increase by roughly 8%. Therefore, if your full retirement age is 66, but you delay taking your benefits until you turn 70, you could essentially give yourself a 32% increase in your Social Security retirement income - and that doesn't even include any cost-of-living increase that may also be included.

Options to Reduce Expenses

In addition to increasing income, you could also consider reducing your expenses if your plan has gone off track. Here too, by spending less, you can essentially help yourself to stretch out the funds that you have.

While some items may be "fixed" expenses - meaning that you may not be able to change the monthly amount - others will be variable. This means that you will have at least some element of control over the amount that you owe.

For example, even on your utilities, you could be more cognizant of what you're using. By turning off lights when you leave a room, not leaving on cell phone and computer chargers 24 / 7, and keeping the heat and air conditioner set at more moderate temperatures, you can reduce your costs. Likewise, by going with a more "basic" cable TV and cell phone plan, you can also lower your monthly bills with these providers. And, shopping around for home, auto, and health insurance each year when your premiums come due can oftentimes net you a great deal of savings.

Also, using coupons and finding sales when shopping for food and clothing, as well as bigger ticket items can save you a tremendous amount of money on a regular basis - and, using a list whenever you shop can help you to avoid "impulse" purchases. This, too, can reduce unplanned expenses.

Can You and Should You Invest More Aggressively?

In some cases, you may wonder if you should invest more aggressively. The answer to that is, it depends. The criteria will be based ultimately on your financial goals, your risk tolerance, your time horizon, and just exactly where it is that you are hoping to go.

The bottom line is that there is no one "right" or "wrong" answer across the board for all investors as a whole - just as there is no one specific route for all people who look at a map. The coordinates that you enter into your GPS device will differ a great deal from that of all other investors - but, the ones that are right for you will ultimately get you to exactly where you want to end up on your retirement journey.

We have reached the end of this book, but your retirement planning journey is just beginning. Just like any type of long journey, planning for retirement must be approached in a similar manner. But this time, the journey could potentially last for 20 or 30 (or more) years. There could also be numerous "detours" and roadblocks along the way - and each of these could cost you in terms of your portfolio. With that in mind, you need to ensure that you don't make any wrong turns.

Having a good, solid plan in place is the best way that you can "map out" your approach for your retirement future - and doing so can be made much easier today with the help of a GPS system. As we saw, the GPS Method takes a "top down" approach, beginning with a look at your overall big picture, and then taking each individual step for how you need to get to your ultimate destination.

Today's retirement has changed a great deal from that of our parents and grandparents. Unlike many years ago, there are little or no guarantees anymore in terms of ongoing income. Now, it is up to individuals to ensure that there will be enough money to generate the income that is needed to pay for necessities in retirement, along with hopefully something more for travel or other luxuries in your golden years.

In order to ensure that you have a good plan in place, it is necessary to put your coordinates into your GPS system. This means estimating how much you will need in terms of expenses during your retirement years.

Once you know how much you will need, you will then have to determine how much income it will take to ensure that you can live the lifestyle that you hope for - and from there, you can work backwards into saving the amount of money that it will require in order to generate that amount of income on an ongoing basis. While there are a number of different options that you can choose from, you will also need to be mindful of a variety of factors when choosing your investment vehicles, including your risk tolerance, your investment time frame, and your overall goals.

As with other types of journeys, the road will not always be smooth. So, the GPS Method will also help you to prepare and plan for certain types of risks that you may run into. These can include pitfalls such as:

- Inflation
- Market Volatility
- Interest Rate Risk
- Global Turmoil

Keep in mind that one of the biggest hurdles that keeps anyone from moving forward and accomplishing their goals is over-thinking things. This is oftentimes referred to as "analysis paralysis." So, when it comes to setting your goals, remember that while you need to be clear about what you want, you also have to make your plan and move forward.

I hope that the GPS Method has given you a new perspective on how to plan for your retirement - as well as on how to think about financial planning as a whole. I also hope it has given you the confidence that you need to move forward, as there is no better time to begin - or continue - than right now.

I wish you success along your journey. If you would like to use the GPS Method to start - or continue - along your path to retirement success, <Contact Me>.